*Facts
and
Phalluses*

Facts & Phalluses

A Collection of Bizarre and
Intriguing Truths, Legends,
and Measurements

Alexandra Parsons

Illustrations by Jennifer Black

St. Martin's Press
New York

Extracts from the Authorized King James Version of the Bible, the rights of which are vested in the Crown in perpetuity within the United Kingdom, are reproduced by permission of Eyre & Spottiswoode Publishers, Her Majesty's Printers, London.

FACTS AND PHALLUSES: A COLLECTION OF BIZARRE AND INTRIGUING TRUTHS, LEGENDS, AND MEASUREMENTS. Copyright © 1989 by Alexandra Parsons. All rights reserved. Printed in the United States of America. No part of this book may be used or reproduced in any manner whatsoever without written permission except in the case of brief quotations embodied in critical articles or reviews. For information, address St. Martin's Press, 175 Fifth Avenue, New York, N.Y. 10010.

Design by Amelia R. Mayone

Library of Congress Cataloging-in-Publication Data

Parsons, Alexandra.
        Facts and phalluses : a collection of bizarre and intriguing truths, legends, and measurements / Alexandra Parsons.
                p.   cm.
        ISBN 0-312-04670-7
        1. Penis—Miscellanea.   2. Penis—Humor.   I. Title.
QP257.P37   1990
591.4'6—dc20   90-37116
                                                                       CIP

First published in Great Britain by Souvenir Press, Ltd

First Edition: November 1990

10 9 8 7 6 5 4 3 2 1

Contents

Facts
and
Phalluses

One

The Human Penis

*T*he purpose of any penis is to deposit sperm somewhere in the vicinity of ripe female eggs. What distinguishes man

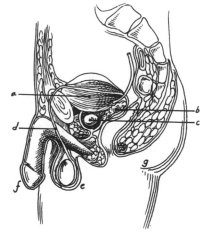

Fig. 1. Reproductive organs (male) in repose:

a) Bladder
b) Seminal vesicle
c) Prostate
d) Deferens duct
e) Testicle
f) Penis
g) Bottom

from the beasts in matters sexual is his year-round enthusiasm for the sexual act, his emotional involvement with his partner and the fact that he enjoys orgasms. The human penis is thought to have developed to its present size in order to excite the female of the species and to enhance the pleasure of the copulatory act.

Time for a *LATIN LESSON*. Popular names for male genitalia in the days of the Roman Empire had a distinctly agricultural flavor:

Testicles	*Fabae*	(beans)
	Mala	(apples)
Penis	*Arbor*	(tree)
	Thysus	(stalk)
	Radix	(root)
	Falx	(sickle)
Semen	*Ros*	(dew)

Size

*M*an has the *LARGEST PENIS* of all the primates. Sizes range from about 1½ inches to an astonishing claim of nearly 19 inches from a star of porno magazines appropriately named Long Dong Silver.

2

There are plenty of myths surrounding *RACE* and *PENIS SIZE*. The most extensive survey on size was carried out by the Kinsey team in America. They found the smallest penis among whites was 1½ inches, while the smallest penis among blacks was 2¼ inches. The largest among whites was 6½ inches, among blacks 6¼ inches. The average size for whites was 4 inches, for blacks it was 4½ inches.

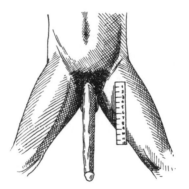

Fig. 2. Believe it or not!

The size of the *MALE NOSE* is supposed to relate directly to the size of the penis.

The size of the *FLACCID PENIS*, fully stretched, is the same as the measurement of the length of the erect penis.

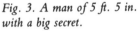

In a study of 80 men—40 of whom had penises measuring 2 to 3½ inches in length and 40 whose penises measured 4 to 4½ inches—the greatest increase from flaccid to erect state occurred in the *MAN WITH THE SMALLEST PENIS* (his penis actually doubled in size). The most insignificant increase—under 2 inches—was recorded in a man whose penis measured 4½ inches. However, the author of the survey admits that conditions were not strictly clinical, that measurement was frequently rushed and as a consequence these statistics cannot be considered definitive—just interesting.

Fig. 3. A man of 5 ft. 5 in. with a big secret.

SHORT MEN ARE SEXY. In yet another fascinating survey, this time of 312 men somewhere in America, the largest penis in the group (5½ inches) belonged to a man just 5ft. 7in. tall.

The size of a man's penis is in no way related to body size. It is entirely a matter of *HEREDITY*.

A boy's penis reaches *ADULT PROPORTIONS* at about the age of 17.

"The man whose Lingaa [penis] is very long will be wretchedly poor. The man whose Lingaa is very thick will ever be very lucky, and the man whose Lingaa is short will be a Rajah." Anangga Rangga

The *BUSHMEN* of the Kalahari desert have semi-erect penises all the time.

5

Changes in the penis during sexual excitement can be measured under laboratory conditions using a mercury-filled rubber tube which is looped around the penis and acts as a *STRAIN GAUGE.*

The urethra increases in both length and *DI-AMETER* during sexual excitement.

Increasing Dimensions

*T*he *CARAMOJA* tribe of Northern Uganda elongate their penises by tying a weight on the end. Sometimes they get so long that the men have to literally tie a knot in them.

"99% of young men and women masturbate occasionally and the 100th conceals the truth." The Encyclopedia of Sexual Behavior, *Havelock Ellis*

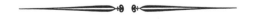

Yes, you can have the operation. Using flaps of skin and tissue from the groin, the penis can be surgically extended. This risky procedure, which can result in a penis up to two times its original length, is undertaken only on patients with *EXTREMELY SHORT* penises.

If you can't face the knife, try chapter II of the *Kama Sutra*, in which you will be advised to rub the member before copulation with tepid water and then anoint it with honey and ginger. This may *STING* and will certainly be *STICKY*.

For cures more desperate than the affliction, we turn to the Arabs, who have developed some very interesting methods of penis enlargement which involve the use of hot pitch, bruised leeches and boiled asses' penises. Such desperate measures should be *AVOIDED*.

Fig. 4. An Arab in a state of some distress.

If all else fails, the *Kama Sutra* claims that an ointment made of the fruit of the koklaksh, whatever that may be, will contract the yoni of an elephant woman for *ONE NIGHT*.

Mutilation

*M*any peoples of the world feel they have to improve on nature with surgery.

AUSTRALIAN ABORIGINALS have been known to slit the penis through to the urethra so that it can be flattened out to resemble the forked penis of the kangaroo.

The *DAYAKS* of Borneo insert, across the top of the penis, a metal rod with balls fixed to the ends. Rich Dayaks use golden balls, poor ones use pebbles.

In some African tribes, only the Chief's eldest son was allowed to procreate. To this end, all the

other sons had a transverse cut made across the
urethra just in front of
the scrotum. The men
were thus not denied
their sexual pleasure but
their semen, and come
to that their urine, never
made it to the tip.
Amongst Europeans this
operation was known
colloquially as *WHIS-
TLE COCK.*

Fig. 5. Next!

The *PEGUANS* of South Burma used to insert
little gold and silver bells under the skin of the
penis.

> Genesis 17:10 *This is my covenant, which ye shall keep between me and you and thy seed after thee; Every man child among you shall be circumcised.*
>
> *11 And ye shall circumcise the flesh of your foreskins; and it shall be a token of the covenant betwixt me and you.*
>
> *14 And the uncircumcised man child whose flesh of his foreskin is not circumcised, that soul shall be cut off from his people.*

JEWS and MUSLIMS and many others remove the foreskin. Circumcision has many detractors. One set of statistics has conclusively proved that circumcised men practically never suffer from cancer of the penis and the wives of circumcised men have a significantly lower rate of cervical cancer. Another set of statistics conclusively proves that the absence or presence of the foreskin is not a significant factor. Circumcision for "hygienic" reasons is increasingly seen as medically unnecessary, dangerous, and rather cruel.

In *ANCIENT ROME* entertainers (musicians, actors, and the like) had holes made in the foreskin and a ring inserted, presumably to stop them taking advantage of their enraptured female fans.

Top athletes in *ANCIENT GREECE*, it is alleged, had their foreskins tied over the top of the glans, to prevent them from weakening themselves by having intercourse.

Fig. 6. All tied up.

POLYNESIANS slit the foreskin lengthwise at puberty.

Some tribes in *AFRICA* and in *POLYNESIA* have practiced semi-castration—the removal of one testicle.

11

TOTAL CASTRATION, now luckily rare, has been practiced throughout the world as a punishment, to produce eunuchs for guard duty at temples and in harems, or to produce singers with fine high voices. Men who have been castrated before puberty retain the hair distribution, voice, and temperament of boys and are, of course, sterile. The effects on a man of castration after puberty vary according to the age and maturity of the individual, but the unfortunate victim will almost always tend to become fat.

Display and Decoration

*I*n some parts of *NEW GUINEA* and *BORNEO* men wear no clothing at all, except for an enormously long and colorful penis sheath made from a gourd. The purpose being to draw attention to the penis, not to hide it.

The males of the *MAMBAS* tribe of the New Hebrides often wrap their penises in yard after yard of calico, winding and folding it into a neat bundle some 17¾ inches long. The purpose is to protect the wearer from the evil eye.

PENIS SHEATHS are a popular form of attire throughout the Third World. Toothpaste tubes, discarded film containers, opened sardine cans and

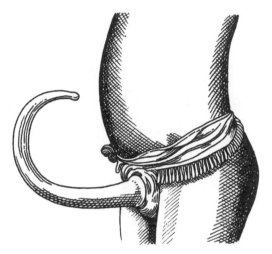

Fig. 7. Penis sheath from New Guinea.

even the leg of a plastic doll have been spotted fulfilling this remarkable role in parts of New Guinea and South Africa.

In fourteenth-century Europe, high-ranking noblemen were permitted to display their *NAKED GENITALS* below a short tunic—their tightly-fitting hose were not joined at the crotch. If their genitals were not of sufficient size to make a fine display dangling enticingly beneath their doublets, they wore a *braquette,* a form-hugging padded falsie made of skin-colored leather.

"Any knight under the rank of a lord, or any other person [is forbidden to wear] any gowne, jaket or cloke unless it be of sufficient length on a man standing upright to cover his privy member and buttokkes." Law passed in 1548 by King Edward VI

In English law *INDECENT EXPOSURE,* which is defined as the display of the penis, flaccid or erect, towards a person of the opposite sex, is an exclusively male offense. It is the most common sexual misdemeanor.

In the fifteenth and sixteenth centuries, European fashion favored the *CODPIECE.* Padded, stiffened, embroidered, bedecked with bows and sometimes with jewels, the codpiece—though it had its origins in modesty—was an explicit sexual signal. The modern double-stitched trouser fly is supposed to be the last vestige of the codpiece.

Protection

The CONDOM was invented by an English army doctor called Colonel Condom. He made it for Charles II from a length of lamb's gut. Condoms (used for birth control and the prevention of venereal disease) were made of animal gut until the early 1840s when a certain Mr. Goodyear discovered how to make them out of rubber.

Fig. 8. State-of-the-art condom.

The most common method of sterilization for men is *VASECTOMY,* in which the vas deferens (the tubes carrying the sperm) are cut. It is quick, simple, and effective. A typical survey reveals that after the operation 74.5 percent of men experienced no difference in their sex drive, 17.9 percent experienced an increase and a paltry 7.9 percent reported a small decrease.

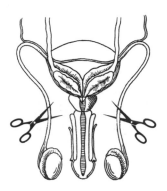

Fig. 9. Snip! Snip!

Sensitivity

*T*he human glans penis is about as sensitive as the *SOLE OF THE FOOT*.

Premature ejaculation is not caused by an overly sensitive penis, but by lack of emotional control. *SO THERE.*

16

Fig. 10. How it's done.

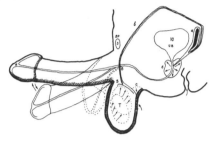

a) Arousal.

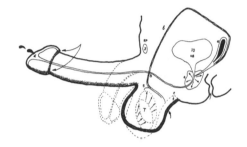

b) In medical parlance, this is called the 'plateau' phase.

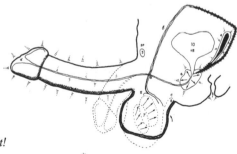

c) This is it!

There is *NO DIFFERENCE* in sensitivity between the circumcised penis and the uncircumcised one.

Prolonging the Pleasure

A few dietary tips from the *Kama Sutra* may come in handy. *MANY EGGS* fried in butter and then immersed in honey will make the member hard for the whole night. It may also make you *SICK*.

CAMELS' MILK mixed with honey produces surpassing vigor and causes the virile member to be on the alert night and day.

Take one part of the juice from pounded onions and mix with two parts of honey. Heat it over a fire until the juice disappears. Let the residue cool and preserve it. Mix one measure with three of water and macerate chickpeas in the fluid for one day and one night. Take this beverage before going to bed and a man will have his member rigid and upright without intermission. This should not be used three nights in succession, and *NEVER IN THE SUMMERTIME.*

If you should happen upon a *CAMEL HUMP,* melt down some of the fat and rub your member with it.

An endorsement for the *ONION* from *The Perfumed Garden*:
The member of Abou el Keiloukh has
    remained erect
For thirty days without a break, because
    he did eat onions.

Fig. 11. Allium sepa

Two

Sperm and Testicles

What is sperm? Basically it is a microscopic bundle of DNA with a little tail on the end of it. The individual sperm of every mammal follows the same basic pattern: tail section, middle, and head. The shape of the head is different for each species, but the size of each individual sperm is the same whether it be a mouse or an elephant.

Sperm are manufactured in the testicles and mixed with seminal fluid, which is a product of the prostate gland. It is this fluid, called semen, which is ejaculated from the penis. Aided by this "carrier" fluid, the sperm attempt to swim up the female reproductive tract and fertilize an egg. The seminal fluids also provide the sperm with energy, and they certainly need it. If you were to multiply the size of a sperm to human proportions and work out in human distances how far a sperm has to travel from

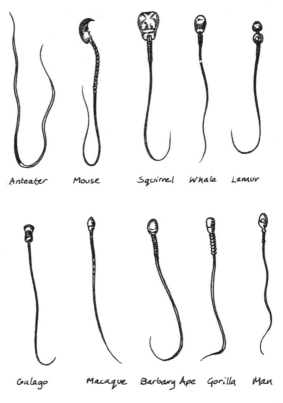

Fig. 12. Single sperm from various sources (to scale).

vagina to egg in a female sheep, for example, it would represent a marathon swim of over 30 miles.

The first people to see sperm through an *OP-TICAL LENS* were a certain Dr. Leeuwenhoek and his associate, a Dr. Hamm. They wrote up their findings and sent them off to the Royal Society of London in November, 1677.

Fig. 13. What some observers saw through the crude microscopes of the 1670s, when sperm were conceived as little men or homunculi.

The amount of sperm a creature produces is relative to the size of the testicles. Relative to its body weight, the *JAPANESE DOLPHIN* has the largest testicles of all.

The testicles of the *BLUE WHALE* are about 2½ feet long and weigh about 110 pounds. The testicles of the *FIN WHALE* weigh a little more than 66 pounds, and those of the *SPERM WHALE* weigh 26½ pounds. The individual spermatozoon of the largest whales is no larger than a man's.

The *RAM* has enormous testicles for its size and it produces about one-fifth to one-half a teaspoon of highly concentrated sperm per ejaculate.

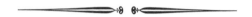

The *PIG* has a pretty impressive set of testicles, and the boar produces a vast amount of seminal fluid—a little more than 2 cups—containing about 85 trillion sperm which takes a leisurely 10 minutes to deliver.

The *HORSE* produces somewhere between 4 and 13 trillion sperm per ejaculate.

The *GUINEA PIG* ejaculates an enormous amount of semen, which then solidifies into a plug, blocking up the female vagina.

One ejaculate from a *BULL* can be diluted out to provide sufficient sperm to artificially inseminate about 300 cows. The testicles of a bull move freely within the scrotum, suspended on a cord called the spermatic cord, which raises the testicles during cold weather and sexual excitement.

Frozen semen for *ARTIFICIAL INSEMI-NATION* of farm animals is stored in plastic straws

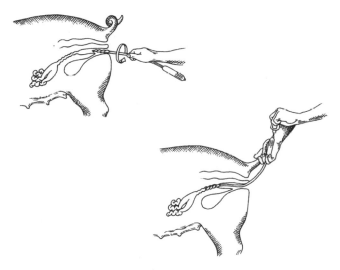

Fig. 14. How to inseminate a pig.

and frozen in liquid nitrogen. Most artificial insemination centers store mainly bull semen, which can be kept for years at temperatures of −110°F. Bull semen sells for an average price of $8 a dose. Top of the line bull semen can command up to $240 a pop. Pig semen is at its most potent when fresh, and is usually collected and delivered within hours. Supplies of frozen sheep and goat semen are also held but they are mainly used to improve breeding lines by introducing new genes from overseas.

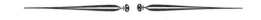

GOURMET CORNER: In Japan, dolphins' testicles are a highly prized treat. In Spain, where anything to do with bulls is an excuse for a party, the traditional inspection of the bulls by the matadors in the morning of a bullfight is marked by an elite social gathering at which bulls' balls are served on rounds of dry toast, accompanied by copious amounts of dry sherry.

In Europe, there is a lower conception rate in wintertime compared to other times of the year. This used to be blamed on heavy, restricting male *UNDERWEAR* reducing fertility. However this theory was completely blown apart when it was discovered that in North America, where it gets as cold and men wrap up just as snugly, the conception rate is at its highest in winter.

Man would live longer without balls. A study of imprisoned castrates in a state penitentiary in America (in the past castration has been a penalty for rape in the United States) proved that the castrates lived on average *13 YEARS LONGER* than their intact counterparts.

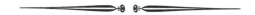

The *SKIN OF THE SCROTUM* is the only part of the body (apart from the eyelid) with little or no subcutaneous fat.

HUMAN SPERM for artificial insemination is kept in small sterile containers in tanks of liquid nitrogen.

Donors of sperm are carefully screened and tested for the *AIDS VIRUS*. The sperm is then held in quarantine for several months and the donor is then retested. Only if the second *AIDS TEST* is negative does the sperm get released to the sperm bank.

The normal *AMOUNT OF SEMEN* produced at one ejaculation by the human male is from one-half to 1 teaspoon (3–5 cubic centimeters), and contains anywhere between 100 and 550 million sperm depending on who is counting.

The pop group *10CC* named themselves after the amount of ejaculate per average orgasm, but they were either misinformed or overly optimistic.

It takes over an *HOUR* for human sperm to travel from the neck of the womb to the last bend of the fallopian tube.

Once inside the female reproductive system, human *SPERM SURVIVES* from three to five days. The sperm of a horse can survive for five-and-a-half days. In some bats, sperm is stored inside the female for up to six months, and can fertilize a newly released egg after a winter of hibernation.

The human male ejaculation is made up of *THREE DISTINCT SPURTS* because of the three main glandular systems that contribute to the discharge. First off the mark are the Cowper's glands, then the prostate, then the testicles, so the last spurt is by far the most potent.

SEMEN is ejaculated as a liquid; it immediately gels and then liquefies again within about five minutes. This is all due to enzyme action and is designed to assist the motility of the sperm.

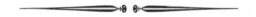

Sperm need to *KEEP COOL*. The difference in *temperature* between the inside of the abdomen and the inside of the scrotum averages out at 1¼°F.

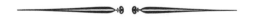

About 85 percent of men have wet dreams. According to Kinsey's research, the frequency of wet dreams is much higher among better-educated men.

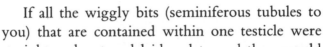

If all the wiggly bits (seminiferous tubules to you) that are contained within one testicle were straightened out and laid end to end they would measure more than *A QUARTER OF A MILE.*

First find the testicle. Testicles that have strayed from the normal path of descent are usually found in the groin, but *MISPLACED TESTICLES* have been found under the skin at the root of the penis and even just in front of the anus.

CLASSICS CORNER: The word *testicles* comes from the Latin for "witness of virility." The origin of the word *prostate* is a phrase in Ancient Greek meaning "guardian," or "one that stands before."

Fig. 15. The Greeks always have a word for it.

Three

Phallic Lore

Because of its obvious association with fertility, the penis has always been a very powerful magic symbol. Phallic symbols are thought to provide the best possible protection against the evil eye.

One of Ancient Egypt's favorite gods was *OSIRIS*, often represented as a menacing bull with three penises.

According to Ancient Hebrew custom, a man would *SWEAR AN OATH* holding in his hand the penis of the man to whom the oath was being sworn.

When the men of the Walibri tribe of central Australia visit other tribes for ceremonial occasions, they *SHAKE PENISES* rather than shake hands.

Some well-known *PHALLIC SYMBOLS* include the Eiffel Tower, Cleopatra's Needle, the Washington Monument, the Empire State Building, and the space shuttle.

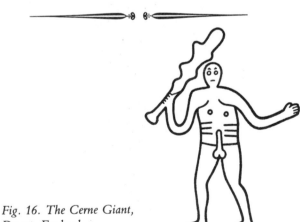

Fig. 16. The Cerne Giant, Dorset, England.

Shintoism is an atavistic religion peculiar to Japan. *PHALLIC SYMBOLS* feature heavily and phallic shrines are dotted all over the countryside.

There is a group of *FOUL-SMELLING MUSHROOMS* called the stinkhorns or, more eruditely, the *phallales,* which closely resemble the

Fig. 17. Relax, it's a mushroom!

male member. In Japan particularly it is a highly prized food, usually served in soup, that is supposed to have a remarkable effect upon a man's virility.

The Ancient Romans worshipped the god *LIBER*, who was in fact not much more than a huge phallic symbol promising luck, wealth, and happiness. They celebrated this god with much enthusiasm—the rites of Liber (hence libertine) lasted a full month.

Modern Hindus *WORSHIP* the lingaa (penis) as a representation of the god Shiva.

Many of the more common *GESTURES* that indicate threat or insult are phallic in origin. The forearm jerk, in which the fist is clenched, the forearm thrust upwards, and the palm of the other hand is slapped against the upper arm, is generally seen as representing a giant phallus that has been thrust into an orifice as far as it will go.

The V-sign showing the back of the hand, and the middle finger jerk, are both obviously phallic in origin, the two-fingered gesture being more common in Europe, the single-finger insult being the style preferred in North America.

At the beginning of the eighteenth century *A BELGIAN LADY* severed the penis from her dearly beloved husband's corpse and treasured it as a relic in a silver casket. She eventually reduced her gruesome souvenir to powder and found it a most efficacious remedy for a number of female complaints.

———————

"A captain told me that when they were rifling the dead bodies of the French gentlemen after the first invasion, they found that many of them had their mistresses' favours tied about their genitories." Familiar letters, *Burton 1627*

———————

Four

Malfunction and Other Disasters

*T*he human penis is an amazingly complex piece of equipment and it is hardly surprising that it sometimes fails to function or becomes exposed to specific diseases.

Impotence

*I*n the human male, an erection is caused by the blood flowing into the spongy erectile tissue of the penis, making it hard and stiff. A malfunction of this vascular system results in impotence. About *10 PERCENT OF ADULT MALES* suffer from impotence at some stage.

As professional groupings go, *ELDERLY DOCTORS* have the highest rate of impotency, and eldery clergymen one of the lowest.

Two of the main causes of temporary impotence are *TIGHT PANTS* and prolonged *CIGARETTE SMOKING*.

Cures for Impotence

*T*he *PENILE IMPLANT* is a very popular cure—about 42,000 of these operations were performed in the United States in 1986. It involves the surgical implantation of a piece of plastic—malle-

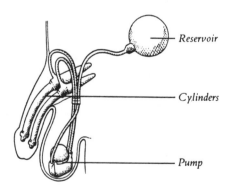

— Reservoir

— Cylinders

— Pump

Fig. 18. Implant implanted.

able enough to be bent out of the way when not required—which keeps the penis permanently hard. More sophisticated and vastly more expensive forms of penile implant use valves and hydraulic fluids and pumps to produce erections to order.

Occasionally plastic penis inserts can cause *CURVATURE OF THE PENIS,* which is corrected surgically by chopping out little wedges of the implant.

The *EREC-AID* is a recent British invention. It is a sheath of thin silicone rubber with a soft

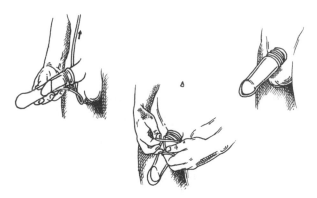

Fig. 19. Using the Erec-Aid.

41

collar at the base. A tube is inserted into this collar and the man sucks on the tube, causing a vacuum inside which causes the penis to engorge with blood and thus become stiff. The man then plugs up the tube and the erection lasts for as long as the vacuum is maintained.

A cure for impotence from Ancient Babylon: The priest beheads a *MALE PARTRIDGE,* and eats its heart. Then he mixes the animal's blood with water, which the impotent patient then drinks.

Hormone Problems

A true *HERMAPHRODITE* is defined as a person who possesses both ovarian and testicular tissue.

In the treatment of children born with intersex problems, the gender of the child is usually decided one way or the other by the physician and then the appropriate surgery and hormone treatments are carried out. This decision must be taken before the child is *18 MONTHS OLD*, otherwise serious psychological problems may occur.

Gossip Columns

A bit of tittle-tattle from the field of battle: The Empire-builder *CHARLEMAGNE* suffered from an irritable bladder caused by an infection of the genitourinary tract. This caused him to get up several times a night to pass water.

Fig. 20. The Holy Roman Emperor after a particularly sleepless night.

———————————————

WILLIAM THE CONQUEROR, for all his bravado, was so apathetic towards women that he was commonly believed to be impotent.

———————————————

FREDERICK THE GREAT—who was reputedly a homosexual—never consummated his marriage to the Princess Elisabeth Christine. It is believed in some circles that he contracted such a severe case of venereal disease in his youth that a total castration had to be performed.

———————————————

The Rise and Fall of *EDWARD GIBBON:* The celebrated expert on the Roman Empire wrote to a friend of "a large prominancy" in his "inexpressibles." It turned out to be a huge fluid sac in his scrotum which was unsuccessfully drained by his surgeon in a series of painful operations. The subsequent infection cost him his life.

———————————————

Among the catastrophes that beset poor *NAPOLEON* was a terrible case of cystitis. He was sometimes observed to rest his head against a tree or wall and moan with pain while urinating.

The great poet, *WALT WHITMAN,* preferred the company of men to women (they used some very tasteful phrases in those days, didn't they?). A post mortem examination revealed that Whitman had probably been born a eunuch.

Rasputin, the Mad Monk of Russia, died an interesting death. He was, in rapid succession, poisoned, shot, raped, castrated, and then drowned. His penis, reportedly a massive 12¾ inches long, was apparently retrieved and carefully preserved in a specially made velvet-lined box. Where is it now?

Curiosities

*I*n some really rare cases *BONE* has formed in the human penis. This painful phenomenon appears to be the result of some sort of accident, so be careful.

Is the *DOUBLE PHALLUS* a myth or a reality? In 1609 a certain Dr. Wecker happened upon a corpse in Bologne with two penises and he described his findings in a learned tome called *De partibus genitalibus,* now sadly out of print.

A WEBBED PENIS—in which a web of skin joins the scrotum to the full length of the underside of the penis—is very uncommon but, luckily, it can be fixed.

An erect penis is a *DELICATE ITEM* that, if hit, can fracture. A fractured penis is defined as a definite tear in the outer casing of the body of erectile tissue known as the *corpus cavernosum.* Men who have suffered such a blow recall hearing a distinct cracking sound followed by an instant collapse of the erection and intense pain.

Of 25 patients suffering from a fracture to the penis, 16 put the cause of the injury down to overenthusiastic masturbation, three admitted it happened during lovemaking, a further three claimed it happened while they slept, and the remaining trio said the injury resulted from *FALLING OUT OF BED*.

Infertility

*A*lthough it only takes one sperm to fertilize an egg, a man whose ejaculate yields *LESS THAN 35 MILLION* sperm is considered infertile.

———————————⟫⊹⊙ ⊙⊹⟪———————————

Some *CAUSES OF INFERTILITY* in males include: high altitude; hot, humid climate; fever; late descent of the testicles into the scrotum (this problem should be dealt with before the child is five); stress; radiation; and some drugs (particularly cannabis and excessive amounts of alcohol).

———————————⟫⊹⊙ ⊙⊹⟪———————————

An interesting cure for infertility: Smear the body with dregs of the *VINEGAR OF WINE,* and let the patient stand in the sun for an hour, and then let him wash himself in hot water.

Priapism

*T*his *UNCOMFORTABLE CONDITION,* named after the Greek god Priapus, is a state of irreversible erection caused by engorgement of the corpus cavernosum, the erectile tissue which runs along the front of the penis.

The Unkindest Cut

*M*en who have suffered from major *ACCI-DENTS* in the crotch area can still lead normal (if sterile) sex lives as long as the penis remains undamaged. A recently monitored group of men who had lost their testicles in the Vietman war were all found to be producing sufficient male hormones from their adrenal glands to bring about both erection and orgasm.

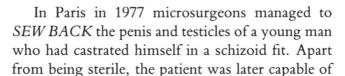

In Paris in 1977 microsurgeons managed to *SEW BACK* the penis and testicles of a young man who had castrated himself in a schizoid fit. Apart from being sterile, the patient was later capable of a normal sex life.

Napoleon's penis was removed from his body at an autopsy performed by a group of French and British doctors trying to establish the true cause of his death.

Men Who Sincerely Want to Be Women

SEX CHANGE operations have been legal since 1952 when a young GI, George Jorgensen, managed to persuade a German surgeon to perform a total castration on him.

In order to turn a *PENIS INTO A VAGINA,* the skin of the penis is retained after the organ itself has been removed and the skin is then inverted, like the finger of a glove, into a surgically created opening. This operation can now be so successful that artificial vaginas have been passed as the real thing by several gynecologists. Psychological adjustment to the operation is another thing altogether.

49

Venereal Diseases

A*NIMALS IN THE WILD* don't get them.

SYPHILIS originated, it is claimed, in the New World and was brought to Europe by Columbus and his crew in 1492. The disease is named after a fictional swineherd who expressed his anger with the gods when his herd was wiped out, and who was subsquently struck down with a vile disease by the unfeeling sun god, Sirus.

CAPTAIN COOK suffered from syphilis, as did Cesare Borgia, Al Capone, Beethoven, Goethe, Hitler, Henry VIII, and Mussolini.

GONORRHEA, characterized by a discharge from the penis, has been around since Biblical times and was named by the Greek physician, Galen, in 150 A.D. The name translates as "the flow of seed."

Age

Old age has nothing to do with it. The idea that older people should not have sexual desires is based on *VICTORIAN PRUDERY* and would have sexual activity entirely confined to reproduction.

———————————⪼⊶ ⊷⪻———————————

Use it or lose it. Men who maintain *ACTIVE SEX LIVES* are more likely to avoid the impotence of old age. Kinsey found one seventy-year-old who still enjoyed seven orgasms a week, and an eighty-eight-year-old who reported a very active sex life with his ninety-year-old wife.

Fig. 21. It's never too late for The Joy of Sex.

51

1 Samuel 18:25 *And Saul said, Thus shall ye say to David, The king desireth not any dowry, but an hundred foreskins of the Philistines, to be avenged of the king's enemies. But Saul thought to make David fall by the hand of the Philistines.*

27 Wherefore David arose and went, he and his men, and slew of the Philistines two hundred men; and David brought their foreskins, and they gave them in full tale to the king, that he might be the king's son in law.

Five

The Animal
Penis

*L*ike human beings, all mammals have a penis with a urethra, through which both urine and semen pass (but never at the same time).

Not every creature is so lucky. Prehistoric animals made do with aligning their cloacae (all-purpose excretory and sexual openings) and hoping for the best. The dinosaur didn't have one, nor did any of his friends and relations. One could say that it all started with the snake, as reptiles were the first forms of life to develop a male cloaca with the ability to protrude and penetrate the female sexual opening.

Most birds still rely upon aligning their cloacae. Some varieties of fish, shellfish, and cephalopods such as the squid and the octopus use an arm or a leg or a handy tentacle to transfer little parcels of sperm into the female. These penis-substitutes are

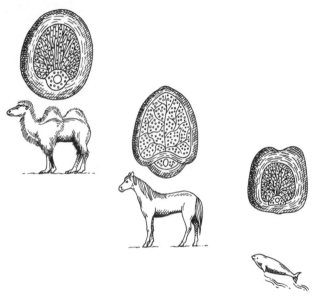

Fig. 22. Cross section through the penis of a camel, a horse, and a Beluga sturgeon. Note the similarities between the camel and the fish.

called gonopods. There are some sea mollusks that forgo close contact altogether and content themselves with squirting their sperm into the water.

Penises come in many different guises—there are hydraulically operated and erectile models and varieties that are fully retractable. Penises come with barbs, with bones, with corkscrew twists, and with knobs on.

Worms

*T*he common *EARTHWORM* is a hermaphrodite with both an erectile penis and a rudimentary vagina. When two earthworms meet, they align themselves head to tail and mate for three or four hours.

The penis of the male *THREADWORM* is shaped like a hooked fork.

Insects

*M*ost male insects have an organ called an aedeagus, often referred to as a penis, which is rather like the finger of a glove. At rest it is pulled inside out and retracted into the lower abdomen.

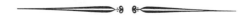

The penis of the male *BEDBUG* is curved, pointed, and very large. As the female bedbug has no vagina, the male just drills his way into the female's abdomen and deposits his sperm in her bloodstream.

The penis of a particularly unsavory species of *MOSQUITO* is long and sharp, enabling the male to rip open female pupae and copulate with the as-yet-unborn.

The male *COCKROACH* has several hook-shaped penises which attach to the female's rear end.

Nature can be perverse. The sexual organs of the male *DRAGONFLY* are in the end of his tail

Fig. 23. Exhausted dragonfly.

and surrounded with hooks with which he grasps the female by the neck. As luck would have it, her sexual opening is not near her neck but at the end of her tail, so the male has been provided with a second penis at the other end of his body. Unfortunately, this second penis produces no sperm, so before copulation the male has to loop his body round, filling the empty sac of his secondary penis from the semen supplied by the first.

The female *PRAYING MANTIS* will bite off the male's head as soon as he mounts and penetrates her. His bottom half will remain on the job as she continues feasting on his shoulders and upper abdomen. It has been established that the brain of the male mantis actually stops him from releasing sperm, so once headless, he can fulfill his destiny, as well as providing his mate with a nutritious, protein-filled meal to sustain her while she lays her eggs.

Just one male *BEE* from the hive will win the right to copulate with the queen. The in-flight mating lasts about two seconds and when the couple separates the male's penis breaks off, remaining inside the queen to ensure no sperm escapes. The male falls to the ground and bleeds to death. Such is life!

Spiders

*P*ity the male spider. He has no penis and he mates at great risk to life and limb. He squeezes sperm from his belly onto his web and picks up the parcel with a special set of antennae, then he scuttles off in search of an interested female. He knows she is interested by the odor she exudes. He also knows

Fig. 24. *Epeira diadema*.

that the female of the species is very likely to *GOB-BLE HIM UP* as a postcoital snack so he has to be very nimble, take her by surprise and run for his life.

Gastropods

*T*he *SNAIL* is a hermaphrodite. It has a (relatively) huge erectile penis and a vagina. Before mating and impregnating one another, two snails will engage in erotic foreplay during which they will fire chalky "love darts" into each other's skin to establish that they are of the same species.

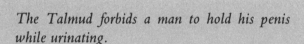

> The Talmud forbids a man to hold his penis while urinating.

SLUGS, also hermaphrodites, circle one another for hours producing huge amounts of slime. The Great Grey slugs, nearly one-half an inch long, copulate while dangling from a rope of slime. Their penises are half their body length.

Fish

*T*here is a species of mating fish called the *FOUR-EYED ANABLEP.* Nature did not make it easy for them. The male's penis may be either on his left side or his right side and the females likewise may have their receptive organs either on the left or the right. So a left-penised male has to search for a right-vagina-ed female and vice versa.

Reptiles

*M*ale *LIZARDS* and *SNAKES* have two penises, which are called hemipenes, one on either side of the body. In repose they are like pockets. When erect, the pockets turn inside out and protrude.

Fig. 25. Copulating snakes.

Hemipenes swell up inside the female. They are double lobed, and a pinky red color prior to ejaculation, and a deep purplish blue thereafter.

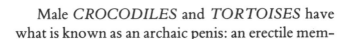

Male *CROCODILES* and *TORTOISES* have what is known as an archaic penis: an erectile member hidden within the cloaca that on arousal is engorged with blood and protrudes. Sperm is not carried within the archaic penis, but on the surface.

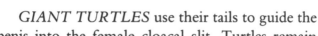

GIANT TURTLES use their tails to guide the penis into the female cloacal slit. Turtles remain locked together for hours.

Speaking of hours, a pair of *PYTHON MOLURUS* or Indian Pythons have been recorded as copulating for a period of 180 days. *DEATH ADDERS* quite routinely take well over a week, and they will not be put off. A snake expert in a learned paper has related how he accidentally dropped a 1,000-watt light bulb on a pair of mating death adders who carried on unperturbed.

Birds

*F*our groups of birds have large erectile members hidden in their cloacae which serve as penises: *DUCKS, SWANS, GEESE,* and a group of *FLIGHTLESS BIRDS* which includes the kiwi, the ostrich, and the emu. Semen is transferred along its outer surface.

The penis of the *WILD MALLARD* is about 1½ inches long.

The penis of the *DOMESTIC DUCK* is a spiral twist about 3 inches long and greyish yellow in color.

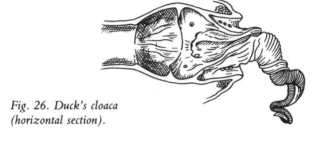

Fig. 26. Duck's cloaca
(horizontal section).

The *COCK* has two tiny erectile papillae—about 2 millimeters in diameter—which protrude from his cloaca during mating. A trained chicken-sexer can spot these in the newly-hatched chick.

The male *EMPEROR PENGUIN* has one orgasm a year.

> *"My impression is that sexual abstinence does not promote the development of energetic, independent men of action, original thinkers or bold innovators and reformers; far more frequently it develops well-behaved weaklings who are subsequently lost in the great multitude."* Sigmund Freud

Spiny Animals and Monotremes

The female *PORCUPINE* comes in heat once a year. In anticipation of this rare event, the male porcupine can sometimes be seen clutching his penis with one hind paw and hobbling around three-legged. When they do mate, they do so with great gusto, each copulation lasting from one to five minutes.

Female *PORCUPINES, HEDGEHOGS,* and *ECHIDNAS* can flatten the spines around their rear ends, thus making the mating process a less prickly affair for the male, who mounts from behind.

The penis of the *ARMADILLO* is about one-third the length of its body.

Fig. 27. The ever-popular nine-banded armadillo.

François Faure (1841–1899), President of France, died while copulating in a whorehouse. The lady, it is alleged, became hysterical and the muscles of her vagina contracted to such an extent that the dead president's member had to be surgically removed.

The penis of the adult *PLATYPUS* is a pretty strange looking appendage. It is about 2¾ inches long and the shaft is armed with several backward-pointing spines. The glans is double-headed, the left-hand side being considerably larger than the right. Each head has four little fronds, each frond containing a branch of the seminal/urethral duct.

Marsupials

*L*ike most marsupials, *KANGAROOS* have a forked, double-headed penis specially designed to fit the female's twin-horned vagina. The marsupial penis has another unique peculiarity in that it hangs behind the scrotum. Kangaroos copulate for hours.

Rats and Bats

*T*he *BAT's* penis is long and bent at an angle to enable him to copulate upside down while clinging

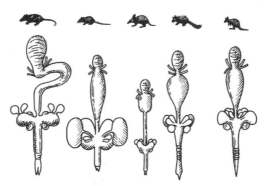

Fig. 28. Various penises of various marsupials.

65

onto the female from behind. Given this precarious positioning it is just as well that, like the elephant, the bat has a motile penis which moves independently of the body, requiring no pelvic thrusting from the owner.

The *ABYSSINIAN BAT's* penis is covered with stiff bristles.

Fig. 29. Common European bat.

The gold medal for recovery after ejaculation goes to a species of desert rat called the *SHAW'S JIRD* which has been observed copulating 224 times in the space of two hours.

HAMSTERS mate facing one another and although the act may be brief, they do it again and again, up to 75 times a day.

Squirrels, Shrews, and Raccoons

*T*he bone in the penis of the *FLYING SQUIRREL* has a saw-edged point.

The *RACCOON's* penis bone is long and thin with a hook at the end and has been used by tailors as a neat little tool to rip out stitching. Mounted in gold and ivory, this appendage has been used as a rather vulgar toothpick.

The *MOLE SHREW* has an S-shaped penis with horny ridges on the glans.

The *GREY SQUIRREL's* penis has a sharp angle to it, whereas the *RED SQUIRREL's* is like a long piece of thread.

> *For the poet, a couple of appropriate rhymes for phallus:*
> callous *hardened skin, or unfeeling*
> thallus *a vegetable structure without vascular tissue in which there is no differentiation into stem and leaves and from which true roots are absent.*

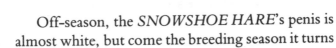

Off-season, the *SNOWSHOE HARE*'s penis is almost white, but come the breeding season it turns bright red.

Cats

A TIGER's penis is about 11¾ inches long, with a conical cap on the end and a lot of little barbs pointing backwards.

The *TOMCAT* has a barbed penis, too. This is because female cats only ovulate when they mate, and the barbs stimulate the vagina and the cervix which in turn brings about the release of the ripe eggs. The cat's penis has a tiny bone at the base.

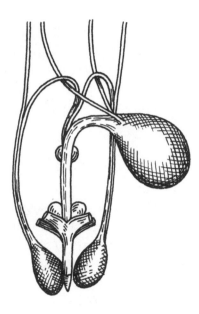

Fig. 30. Genital organs of a tomcat.

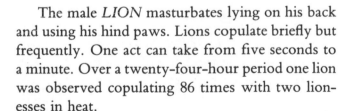

The male *LION* masturbates lying on his back and using his hind paws. Lions copulate briefly but frequently. One act can take from five seconds to a minute. Over a twenty-four-hour period one lion was observed copulating 86 times with two lionesses in heat.

> *First find the cat. This is a cure for burns from the* Syriac Book of Medicine: *Boil bean flour and the crusts of bread with a cat's penis and smear over the burn.*

Dogs

*T*he dog's penis has a narrow base with a small bone to stiffen it and a very large, soft glans. This is because when a dog mates it will mount the bitch and thrust away for 20 to 30 seconds, and then cock his leg over and turn 180 degrees, so that the dog and bitch are still locked together but *FACING DIFFERENT DIRECTIONS*. They will stay this way for 15 to 30 minutes.

Aquatic Mammals

*W*HALES and *DOLPHINS* are very gentle lovers, caressing one another with their fins and stroking each other with their bodies. Actual copulation lasts only a few seconds, but it may be repeated a number of times within a period of about half an hour.

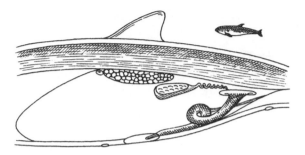

Fig. 31. Sexual organs of a male porpoise.

A *WHALE*'s penis is very similar to that of the bull and the goat in that it resembles a thin hard rope of fibrous tissue. In the larger whales, the penis can be as long as 3¼ yards with a diameter of 11¾ inches. The whale mates once a year, and for the rest of the time his huge appendage is retracted into the penis slit and lies coiled inside the skin of the abdomen.

Let's hear it for the *WALRUS!* He has an exceptionally large penis and the bone in it, which can be up to 24½ inches long, is the longest of any living mammal and is a prized find among seal hunters who use this blunt instrument to club seal pups to death. The male walrus is potent for only three months of the year, January, February, and March.

71

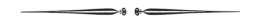

Most species of *SEA LION* copulate for about 20 minutes. After copulation they have been observed immersing their backsides in the sea to cool off.

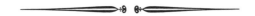

The penis of the *SOUTH AMERICAN SEA LION* consists mainly of a bone which reaches from the base to the tip of the glans and is covered by a thin layer of tissue. The bone is about 5¾ inches long and about three-quarters of an inch in diameter.

Question: What is long, pointed, surprisingly thick, and bright red?
Answer: The penis of the *SEA OTTER*.

The *BEAVER*'s penis is situated within his cloaca and is positioned so that beavers can mate face to face. The act of copulation lasts about three minutes.

The bone in the *ELEPHANT SEAL*'s penis is about 13¾ inches long and three-quarters of an inch wide.

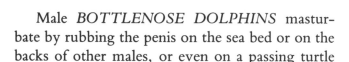

Male *BOTTLENOSE DOLPHINS* masturbate by rubbing the penis on the sea bed or on the backs of other males, or even on a passing turtle or shark.

Down on the Farm

The penis of a *PIG* is a stiff coil, which, when erect, resembles a corkscrew about 17¾ inches long with a counter-clockwise twist. The cervix of the sow has a similar bore, so the pigs are literally locked together during their lengthy coitus. The catheter used for artificial insemination of sows has the same twist.

The *BULL* copulates in one thrust which lasts less than a second. The penis of the bull is bright red. It is like a rope of fibrous tissue which, when dried, becomes springy. Dried bulls' penises are called pizzles and have been traditionally used as whips and riding crops.

Bulls have a hydraulic penis; small muscles around the pelvis contract and squeeze it out from its hiding place under the skin of the abdomen where it lies coiled into an S-shape.

———————————————

The urethras of the *RAM* and the *GOAT* project 2¾ to 4 inches beyond the end of the penis like a worm. Their penises are vascular and full erection occurs only during sexual excitement, but each time the animal urinates there is a slight erection.

Fig. 32. Ram's penis.

Big Game

*T*he *PYGMY HIPPOPOTAMUS* copulates in the water. He has a recurved or backward-facing penis which enables him to "mark" his territory simultaneously with both urine and feces. Charming.

Fig. 33. Hippo's backside.

It pays to advertise. The growth of antlers in the *DEER* family is directly related to the growth of the penis, as antler growth is governed by hormone secretions from the testicles. Male deer masturbate by rubbing their antlers on a tree or on the ground, which swiftly produces an erection and ejaculation.

Male *ELEPHANTS* masturbate using their trunks. Their penises are motile, meaning that once inserted, the penis itself does all the thrusting required, the bull elephant remaining calmly balanced on his hind legs with his front legs resting gently on the female's back. An elephant can only get an erection during the mating season.

The *BUFFALO* has a pointed penis.

The *RHINOCEROS,* which incidentally is monogamous, has a penis nearly two feet long.

Primates

*T*he penis of most mammals is protected within a sheath from which it emerges when engorged with blood. Not so the primates. They (and they share this peculiarity with the bat) have a pendulant penis that is not enclosed in a sheath of skin.

For their size, *GORILLAS* have very small penises. The average male gorilla weighs about 550

pounds—over a quarter of a ton—but his penis is practically hidden in the surrounding fur, and projects stiffly all the time, thanks to a penis bone about three-quarters of an inch long and 1 inch in diameter. One of the main reasons why the gorilla's penis is so small is because he doesn't use it very often. Gorillas copulate about once a year if they are lucky. The females are only in heat for about six days within a four-year cycle.

The erect penis of the male *CHIMPANZEE* is about 3 inches in length and bright pink. Chimps are supple enough to perform fellatio on themselves, and the practice is common. They have a small bone in the penis and they mate regularly throughout the year.

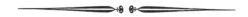

The *MANDRILL,* a colorful variety of African baboon, has a scarlet penis and a bright blue scrotum.

BABOONS and *MACAQUES* have no breeding season and seem to indulge in sex frequently, particularly in the early mornings and at nightfall when it is quiet and peaceful. The act itself is brief and rarely lasts for more than 15 seconds.

The penis of the *ORANGUTAN* is bright pink and about 1½ inches long when erect. Orangutans copulate hanging upside down, not from chandeliers, but from tree branches.

Errol Flynn was reputed to have a huge penis. Those who knew about such things say that the top of his penis could be glimpsed emerging from his waistband through his open-to-the-waist ruffled shirts.

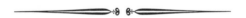

The female *HOWLER MONKEY* is often mistaken for the male, as her clitoris is the same size as his penis. This confusion has led to erroneous reports of homosexuality among monkeys.

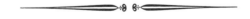

Primates

Homosexuality among *SPIDER MONKEYS* is likely to be fairly rare as the male's penis is covered with sharp, backward-pointing horny barbs.

Bibliography

The Bible: Authorized King James Version of the Bible.

Birds: Their structure and function A. S. King and J. McLelland. *Eastbourne, England:* Baillière and Tindall, 1984.

Body Packaging Julian Robinson. The Watermark Press, 1988.

The Book of Cures Camilla Sendal, ed. *Sydney:* Collins Australia, 1988.

Encyclopedia of Sexual Behavior Havelock Ellis.

Gestures: Their origins and distribution Desmond Morris, Peter Collett, Peter Marsh, and Marie O'Shaughnessy. *London:* Jonathan Cape, 1979.

Introductory Mycology C. J. Alexopoulus. *New York:* John Wiley & Sons, 1952.

Male Infertility Richard D. Amelar, MD; Lawrence Dubin, MD; and Patrick C. Walsh, MD. *Eastbourne, England:* W. B. Saunders Co., 1977.

The Male Member Kit Schwartz. *New York:* St. Martin's Press, 1985.

Man Richard J. Harrison and William Montagna. *Des Moines:* Meredith Corporation.

The Mating Game Robert Burton. *New York:* Elsevier/Phaidon, 1976.

Medical Biographies. Norman: University of Oklahoma Press, 1952.

Monotreme Biology vol. 20 part 1 M. L. Augee, ed. 1978.

The Natural History of Mammals François Bourlière, trans. H. Parshley. *London:* George Harrap, 1955.

Reproduction in Mammals Book 8, Human Reproduction C. R. Austin and R. V. Short FRS, eds. *New York:* Cambridge University Press.

The Sex Life of Wild Animals Eugene Burns. *New York:* Fawcett World Library.

Sex Link Hy Freedman. *New York:* M. Evans and Co., 1977.

Sexual Myths and Fallacies James Leslie McCary. *New York:* Van Nostrand Reinhold Co., 1971.

Sexual Practices Edgar Gregerson. *London:* Mitchell Beazley, 1982.

Studies in the Psychology of Sex Havelock Ellis.

Whales E. J. Slijper, trans. A. J. Pomerans. *London:* Hutchinson & Co., 1962.

Bibliography

Journals

British Journal of Urology
Journal of Urology
Medical Journal of Puerto Rico
Plastic Reconstructive Surgery
Scandinavian Journal of Urology

The Vietnamese unit of currency is known as the Dong.